MIAMI
Heat

BY K. C. KELLEY

Published by The Child's World®
1980 Lookout Drive • Mankato, MN 56003-1705
800-599-READ • www.childsworld.com

Acknowledgments
The Child's World®: Mary Berendes, Publishing Director
Red Line Editorial: Editorial direction
The Design Lab: Design
Amnet: Production

Design elements: PhotoDisc, Viorika Prikhodko/
iStockphoto

Photographs ©: David Santiago, El Nuevo Herald/
AP Images, cover, title; David Santiago/AP Images, 5,
25; Wilfredo Lee/AP Images, 6, 13; Alan Greth/AP
Images, 9; Phelan M. Ebenhack/AP Images, 10; Donna
McWilliam/AP Images, 17; Todd Essick/AP Images, 18;
J. Pat Carter/AP Images, 21; Matt York/AP Images, 22;
Alan Diaz/AP Images, 26

ISBN 978-1623235017
LCCN 2013931368

Printed in the United States of America
Mankato, MN
July, 2013
PA02171

About the Author

K. C. Kelley has written dozens
of books on basketball, football,
baseball, and other sports for
young readers. K. C. used to
work for NFL Publishing and has
covered several Super Bowls.
He likes to watch any basketball
game, but his favorite team is the
Los Angeles Lakers.

Table *of* Contents

Go, Heat!

Miami has lots of fun things to do. You can go to the beach. You can look at beautiful pink-and-yellow buildings. You can take a boat ride or go fishing. Or . . . you can enjoy great basketball action! Seeing the Miami Heat is one of the hottest things to do in the team's sunny hometown. Let's get out of the heat and go meet the Heat!

Dwyane Wade has led the Heat to new heights.

Who Are the Heat?

The Miami Heat play in the National Basketball Association (NBA). They are one of 30 teams in the NBA. The NBA includes the Eastern Conference and the Western Conference. The Heat play in the Southeast Division of the Eastern Conference. The winner of the Eastern Conference plays the winner of the Western Conference in the **NBA Finals**. The Heat won back-to-back NBA titles in 2012 and 2013.

The Heat's LeBron James is a one-of-a-kind superstar.

Where They Came From

The Miami Heat first played in 1988. They were added to the NBA that year along with the Charlotte Hornets. The Hornets are now called the Pelicans. They play in New Orleans. The Heat didn't do well in their early years. In fact, they only had one winning record in their first six seasons. The team worked through it, though. By the mid-1990s, the Heat were in the **playoffs** almost every season!

Miami's Sherman Douglas (11) drives to the hoop in 1990.

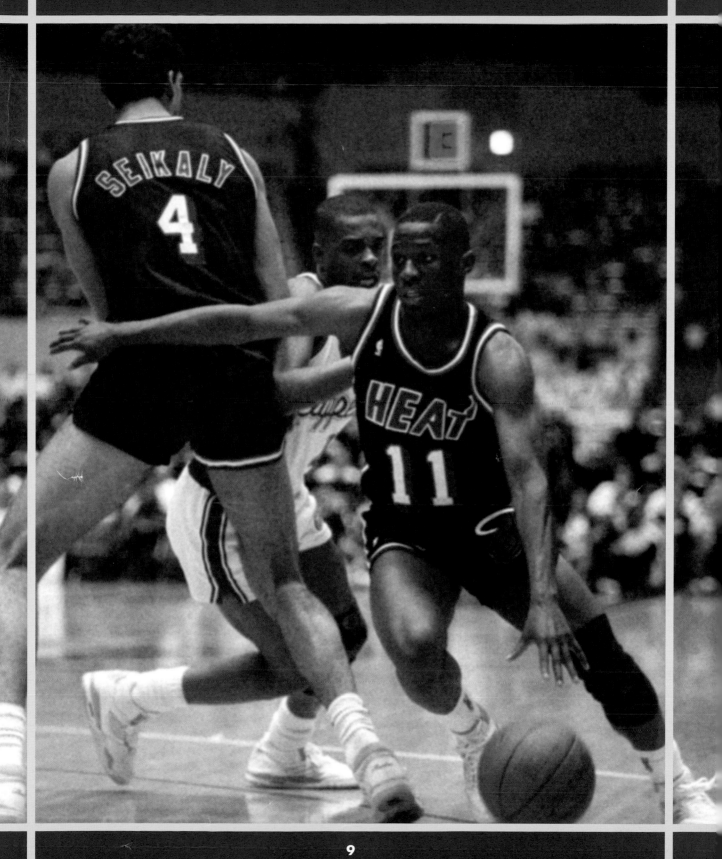

Who They Play

The Heat play 82 games each season. That's a lot of basketball! They play every other NBA team at least once each season. They play teams in their division and conference more often. Since 1989, the Heat have had a big **rivalry** with the Orlando Magic. Both of those teams play in Florida. The Heat and the Los Angeles Lakers became rivals in the 2000s. They were often two of the best teams in the NBA.

Games between the Heat and the Magic are always hot tickets.

Where They Play

The Heat play their home games at the American Airlines Arena. This arena can hold more than 19,000 basketball fans. Basketball isn't the only thing that happens there. When the Heat aren't playing, the arena holds concerts and even professional wrestling shows. The Heat's NBA championship banners hang high over the floor.

The American Airlines Arena is a great place to watch a basketball game.

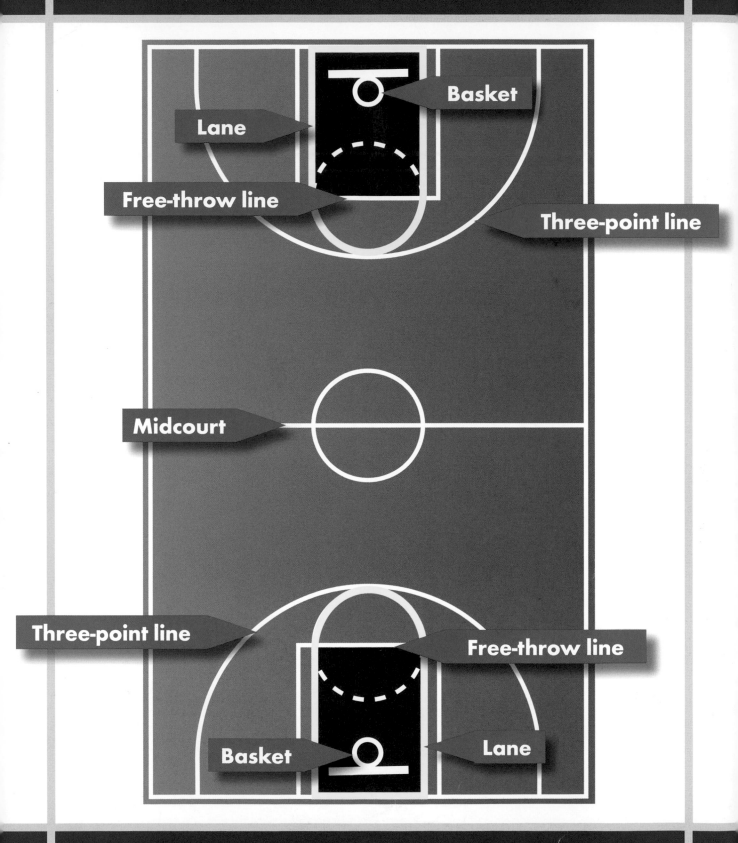

Basket

Lane

Free-throw line

Three-point line

Midcourt

Three-point line

Free-throw line

Basket

Lane

The Basketball Court

Basketball is played on a court made of wood. An NBA court is 94 feet (29 m) long. A painted line shows the middle of the court. Other lines lay out the free-throw area. The space below each basket is known as the "lane." The baskets at each end are 10 feet (3 m) off the ground. The metal rims of the baskets stick out over the court. Nylon nets hang from the rims.

Big Days

The Miami Heat have had many great moments in their history. Here are three of the greatest:

1992: In only their fourth season, the Heat made the playoffs.

2006: The Heat won their first NBA championship. They beat the Dallas Mavericks in six games in the NBA Finals.

2013: The Heat won their second NBA title in two years! They beat the San Antonio Spurs in an exciting seven-game series. One year earlier Miami beat the Oklahoma City Thunder in five games.

Coach Pat Riley helps hold up the 2006 NBA championship trophy.

Tough Days

The Heat can't win all their games. Some games or seasons don't turn out well. The players keep trying to play their best, though. Here are some of the toughest times in the team's history:

1989: It was a tough start. In their first season, the Heat struggled. They won only 15 games.

2008: What happened? After making the playoffs in 2007, the Heat won only 15 games in 2008. They were doing better by 2009, however.

2011: The star-studded Heat lost to the Dallas Mavericks in the NBA Finals. Miami was favored after adding LeBron James and Chris Bosh that season.

The Heat lost to a lot of teams in 1988–89, including the Los Angeles Lakers.

Meet the Fans

Miami fans love their Heat basketball. In fact, fans all over South Florida cheer for the team. Famous celebrities can often be found at Heat games, too. At games, fans enjoy watching the team's dancers and cheerleaders. The fans often wear bright orange clothes. Red, orange, white, and black are the Heat's colors. The team holds lots of contests to help fans share in the fun!

These fans really love the Heat!

Heroes Then . . .

Center Alonzo Mourning played for Miami early and later in his career. His size and strength made him a star on **defense**. He also helped the team win its first NBA title in 2006. Mourning retired as the team's all-time scoring leader. **Guard** Tim Hardaway played for the Heat from 1996 to 2001. Miami made the playoffs every year he was with the team! He was great at passing the ball to teammates. He could also shoot well from **three-point range**. In 2004, the Heat traded for massive center Shaquille O'Neal. He played a key role in Miami's 2006 NBA title. He was very hard to stop when he got the ball near the basket.

Center Shaquille O'Neal dominated under the hoop.

Heroes Now . . .

The Miami Heat already had one of the NBA's best players in guard Dwyane Wade. In 2010 they added two more superstars in **forwards** LeBron James and Chris Bosh. All three are great at **offense**. "D-Wade" is great at driving to the basket to score. James is an all-around spectacular player. He can dribble, pass, shoot, leap, and defend with the best of the NBA. Bosh is often among the NBA's highest scoring players each season, too. This trio led the Heat to the 2012 and 2013 NBA titles.

LeBron James (6) and Dwyane Wade (3) are a dynamite duo.

Wristband

Jersey

Shorts

Knee brace

Socks

Basketball shoes

Gearing Up

Miami Heat players wear the team's uniform and special basketball sneakers. Some wear other pads to protect themselves. Check out this picture of Chris Bosh and learn about what NBA players wear.

THE BASKETBALL

NBA basketballs are made of leather. Several pieces are held together with rubber edges. Inside the leather ball is a hollow ball of rubber. This is filled with air. The leather is covered with little bumps called "pebbles." The pebbles help players get a good grip on the ball. The basketball used in the Women's National Basketball Association (WNBA) is slightly smaller than the men's basketball.

Chris Bosh rocks Miami's stylish white uniforms.

Note: All numbers shown are through the 2012–13 season.

HIGH SCORERS

These players have scored the most points for the Heat.

PLAYER	POINTS
Dwyane Wade	16,453
Alonzo Mourning	9,459

HELPING HAND

Here are Miami's all-time leaders in **assists**.

PLAYER	ASSISTS
Dwyane Wade	4,049
Tim Hardaway	2,867

CLEANING THE BOARDS

Rebounds are a big part of the game. Here are the Heat's best rebounders.

PLAYER	REBOUNDS
Udonis Haslem	5,157
Alonzo Mourning	4,807

MOST THREE-POINT SHOTS MADE

Shots taken from behind a line about 23 feet (7 m) from the basket are worth three points. Here are the Heat's best at these long-distance shots.

PLAYER	THREE-POINT BASKETS
Tim Hardaway	806
Eddie Jones	712

COACH

Who coached the Heat to the most wins?

Pat Riley, 454

GLOSSARY

assists passes to teammates that lead directly to making baskets

center a player (usually the tallest on the team) who plays close to the basket

defense when a team doesn't have the ball and is trying to keep the other team from scoring

forwards two tall players who rebound and score near the basket

guard one of two players who set up plays, pass to teammates closer to the basket, and shoot from farther away

NBA Finals the seven-game NBA championship series, in which the champion must win four games

offense when a team has the ball and is trying to score

playoffs a series of games between 16 teams that decides which two teams will play in the NBA Finals

rebounds missed shots that bounce off the backboard or rim and are grabbed by another player

rivalry an ongoing competition between teams that play each other often, over a long time

three-point range an area beyond a line that's about 23 feet (7 m) from the basket, where shots are worth three points instead of two

BOOKS

Frisch, Aaron. *Miami Heat*. Mankato, MN: Creative Paperbacks, 2012.

Hareas, John. *Championship Teams*. New York: Scholastic, 2010.

Smallwood, John N. *Megastars*. New York: Scholastic, 2011.

Yasuda, Anita. *LeBron James*. New York: Weigl, 2012.

WEB SITES

Visit our Web page for links about the Miami Heat and other NBA teams:
childsworld.com/links

Note to Parents, Teachers, and Librarians: We routinely verify our Web links to make sure they are safe and active sites. So encourage your readers to check them out!

INDEX